# Country File
# Spain

**Ian Graham**

W
FRANKLIN WATTS
LONDON · SYDNEY

Revised and updated 2005

Franklin Watts
96 Leonard Street, London
EC2A 4XD

Franklin Watts Australia
Level 17/207 Kent Street
Sydney NSW 2000

COUNTRY FILE: SPAIN produced for Franklin Watts by
Bender Richardson White, PO Box 266, Uxbridge, UK.
*Editor:* Lionel Bender
*Designer and Page Make-up:* Ben White
*Picture Researcher:* Cathy Stastny
*Cover Make-up:* Mike Pilley, Radius
*Production:* Kim Richardson

*Graphics and Maps:* Stefan Chabluk

*Consultant:* Dr Terry Jennings, a former geography teacher
and university lecturer. He is now a full-time writer of
children's geography and science books.

A CIP catalogue record for this book is available
from the British Library.

ISBN 0 7496 6415 0

Dewey classification 914.6

Printed in China

## Picture Credits

Pages 1: PhotoDiscInc/Emma Lee/Life File. 3: PhotoDisc
Inc/Emma Lee/Life File. 4: James Davis Travel
Photography. 7: PhotoDisc Inc/Emma Lee/Life File. 8:
James Davis Travel Photography. 9: Eye
Ubiquitous/P.Thompson. 10: PhotoDisc Inc/Neil Beer.
11: Lionheart Books. 12: James Davis Travel Photography.
13: Eye Ubiquitous/Mike Feeney. 14: Eye
Ubiquitous/Mike Feeney. 15: James Davis Travel
Photography. 16: Eye Ubiquitous/S.Miller. 18: Eye
Ubiquitous/D.Cumming. 19 Eye Ubiquitous/D.Cumming.
20: Eye Ubiquitous/Paul Seheult. 21: Spanish Tourist
Office, London. 22 top: Spanish Tourist Office, London.
22 bottom: Eye Ubiquitous/John Hulme. 24: Eye
Ubiquitous/Barry Denyer. 25: Eye Ubiquitous/Bob
Battersby. 27: Lionheart Books. 28–29: Eye
Ubiquitous/Mike Feeney. 30: PhotoDisc Inc/Emma
Lee/Life File. 31:PhotoDisc Inc/Neil Beer.

Cover Photo: James Davis Travel Photography.

### Note to parents and teachers
Some of the websites listed in this book are in Spanish
but most have the option to view in English. Every effort
has been made by the Publishers to ensure that the
websites in this book are suitable for children, that they
are of the highest educational value, and that they
contain no inappropriate or offensive material. However,
because of the nature of the Internet, it is impossible to
guarantee that the contents of these sites will not be
altered. We strongly advise that Internet access is
supervised by a responsible adult.

## The Author
Ian Graham is a full-time writer and
editor of non-fiction books. He has
written more than 100 books for children.

# Contents

# Welcome to Spain

The Kingdom of Spain occupies most of the Iberian peninsula at the south-western corner of Europe. Spain also controls the Canary Islands, the Balearic Islands and five areas on and off the coast of Morocco. The British colony of Gibraltar occupies a tiny peninsula on Spain's south coast.

Spain is one of the most mountainous countries in Europe. It shares common borders with Portugal, France, the tiny Pyrenean state of Andorra and Gibraltar. Its cool north coast skirts the Bay of Biscay. Most of its warmer south and east coast lies on the Mediterranean Sea.

Spain has influenced other countries for over 500 years. It was the first European country to establish an overseas empire, mainly in America. Today, Spain is best known as one of the world's most popular holiday destinations.

**DATABASE**

## Regionalism

Spain's regions have maintained their distinctive identities and customs despite determined attempts to crush them during the Franco era (1936–75). Since then, the diverse cultures, languages and customs of the regions have been encouraged and celebrated.

Calle Alcalá in the capital city, Madrid. The streets are filled with shops, offices, pedestrians and traffic. ▼

ATLANTIC OCEAN

Bay of Biscay

FRANCE

44°N

*Golfe de Gascogne*

La Coruña

Gijón

Oviedo

Santander

Bilbao

San Sebastián

PYRENEES

ANDORRA

*Golfe du Lion*

42°N

Santiago de Compostela

CORDILLERA CANTABRICA

Villablino

Vitoria

Pamplona

Figueres

Gerona

Vigo

Orense

SIERRA CABRERA

León

*Esla*

Logroño

COSTA BRAVA

Burgos

Zaragoza

*Ebro*

Lérida

Tarrasa

Barcelona

40°N

Valladolid

*Duero*

SISTEMA IBERICO

Tarragona

Zamora

Salamanca

Segovia

Guadalajara

□ MADRID

Menorca

Mallorca

Palma

S P A I N

Toledo

*Tajo*

MESETA CENTRAL

Valencia

BALEARIC ISLANDS

38°N

Cáceres

Trujillo

MONTES DE TOLEDO

*Júcar*

Alcira

Ibiza

Ibiza

Badajoz

*Guadiana*

Ciudad Real

Albacete

Alcoy

Formentera

Puertollano

Alcaráz

Alicante

Nerva

SIERRA MORENA

Linares

SIERRA DE SEGURA

Murcia

Córdoba

*Guadalquivir*

Martos

Lorca

Cartagena

Huelva

Sevilla

Granada

Cerro de Mulhacén

Almería

M E D I T E R R A N E A N   S E A

Jerez de la Frontera

Antequera

SIERRA NEVADA

36°N

*Golfo de Cadiz*

Cádiz

Málaga

Marbella

COSTA DEL SOL

Gibraltar

*Strait of Gibraltar*

Ceuta

ALGERIA

Melilla

34°N

PORTUGAL

Legend:
- Mountains
- △ Mountain peak
- Grassland and farming
- □ Capital
- ○ Major city
- Country boundary

0 — 200 Miles

0 — 200 Kilometres

CANARY ISLANDS

N W E S

Lanzarote

Arrecife

La Palma

Santa Cruz de La Palma

Tenerife

Santa Cruz de Tenerife

Fuerteventura

Puerto del Rosario

Gomera

△ Teide

Las Palmas

Hierro

Gran Canaria

M O R O C C O

8°W     6°W     4°W     2°W     0°     2°E

# The Land

**M**ost of the central part of Spain consists of a great, almost treeless, plateau called the Meseta (meaning Tableland) Central. The Meseta is crossed by the Central Sierras mountain range.

The Meseta Central plateau is framed by a series of mountain ranges. The Cantabrian mountains (Cordillera Cantábrica) lie to the north, the Sierra Morena to the south and the Iberian Cordillera (Sistema Ibérico) to the east. The Pyrenees stretch for 440 kilometres across the neck of the peninsula and separate it from France.

The highest mountain on Spanish territory is Teide Peak on Tenerife, in the Canary Islands. It rises to an altitude of 3,751 metres. On the Spanish mainland, the highest peak is Mulhacén, near the south coast. It rises to 3,481 metres.

## Average Rainfall

| Average Annual Rainfall | |
|---|---|
| in | cm |
| above 80 | above 200 |
| 40–80 | 100–200 |
| 20–40 | 50–100 |
| 10–20 | 25–50 |

Madrid○

The north-west of Spain is the wettest, with an annual rainfall of about 965 mm.

## Wildlife

Spain has a rich and varied animal and plant life. Its closeness to Africa means that it is home to many African species, including an occasional invasion by desert locusts.

**Mammals:**
European wolf, brown bear, barbary ape (in Gibraltar), wild boar, ibex, wild goat, red deer, fallow deer, pardel lynx, Egyptian mongoose, blind mole, red squirrel, dormouse, weasel, stone marten, genet, bat, rabbit, hare, fox and monk seal.

**Birds:**
Imperial eagle, golden eagle, Bonnelli's eagle, booted eagle, griffon vulture, black vulture, peregrine falcon, marsh harrier, woodpecker, eagle owl, barn owl, buzzard, red kite, black-shouldered kite, white stork, goshawk, azure-winged magpie, golden oriole and pheasant.

**Reptiles and amphibians:**
Gecko, fire salamander, marbled newt, ocellated lizard, smooth snake, whip snake, green tree-frog, midwife toad and chameleon.

Rainfall and snow-melt on Spain's mountains give rise to an extensive river system. Major rivers include the Tagus (Spanish *Tajo*), Ebro, Duero, Guadiana and Guadalquivir. Of these, only the Ebro drains into the Mediterranean Sea. All the others flow into the Atlantic Ocean.

▲ A hilltop village and backdrop of mountains near the east coast of Spain. Here the summers are hot and the land becomes parched.

## Climate

Spain has a varied climate resulting from its size, its mountain ranges and its closeness to both the Atlantic Ocean and the Sahara Desert. Northern Spain has a temperate and humid climate. The rest of the country has a more Mediterranean type of climate – cooler and drier inland, hotter and more humid around the coast.

The mountain ranges influence the climate by casting 'rain shadows' downwind, creating large arid areas. The Canary Islands, off the coast of north-west Africa, have a summer-like sub-tropical Atlantic climate all year round. The Balearic Islands, off Spain's east coast, have mild winters and hot, dry summers.

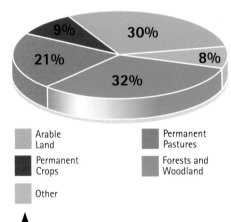

Arable Land — Permanent Pastures — Permanent Crops — Forests and Woodland — Other

▲ Land use in Spain. Less than 10 per cent of land is urban, but much of the rest is too hilly or dry to grow crops.

# The People

- 4%
- 6%
- 17%
- 73%

- Spanish or Castilian
- Catalan
- Basque
- Galician

▲ After Castilian, the most widely spoken language in Spain is Catalan, followed by Galician and Basque.

A fruit and vegetable stall in Málaga, where Spaniards speak Castilian. ▼

S pain has a population of approximately 40 million people. They are the descendants of the many peoples who have invaded and settled in Spain throughout recorded history.

Celts, Basques, Phoenicians, Greeks, Carthaginians, Romans, Vandals, Visigoths and North Africans have all made their home in the Iberian peninsula at different times. Each new wave of settlers fought for land and defended it against new invaders. As a result, Spain became a patchwork of different kingdoms until the Romans brought them within a single political system in the 3rd century BCE. The Visigoths, who invaded the country from Germany in the 5th century, imposed Catholicism on the population. Moors (Muslim Arabs from North Africa) invaded and controlled the country until the end of the 15th century. Marriages between the royal families of the old kingdoms and the defeat of the Moors finally unified the country.

## Language
Most people in Spain speak the country's official language, Castilian. About 75 per cent of the population speak it as their first language. The Spanish constitution allows the regions to have their own languages and dialects. In Catalonia, the Balearic Islands and Navarre, Catalan is spoken. Basque is spoken in the Basque Country, Aragonese in Aragon, and Galician in Galicia.

Other minority languages without official status are protected by law. Most people who speak a regional language also speak Castilian as a second language.

There are significantly more women than men in Spain's population.

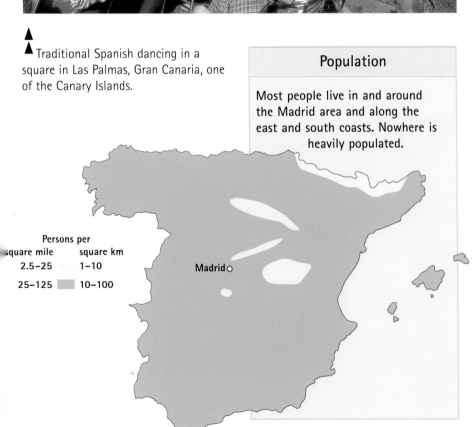

Traditional Spanish dancing in a square in Las Palmas, Gran Canaria, one of the Canary Islands.

## Population

Most people live in and around the Madrid area and along the east and south coasts. Nowhere is heavily populated.

Persons per

| square mile | square km |
|---|---|
| 2.5–25 | 1–10 |
| 25–125 | 10–100 |

Madrid ○

## Web Search ▶▶

▶ http://www.in-spain.info
*All about Spain and its people.*

▶ http://www.spain.info
*Spanish Tourist Office information about the people and culture of Spain.*

▶ http://www.worldinfo zone.com/country. php?country=Spain
*Information about the population and languages of Spain.*

# Urban and Rural Life

22%

78%

■ Percentage of Population
Living in Urban Areas

■ Percentage of Population
Living in Rural Areas

Three out of every four people live in towns and cities.

**M**ore than three-quarters of the people in Spain live in towns and cities. Until the 1950s, the population was largely rural and heavily dependent on agriculture. Increasing industrialization prompted people to move from the countryside into the towns and cities to look for work in the new industries.

This process of urbanization occurred later in Spain than in the rest of Europe. In 1953, only 53 per cent of the population was urban. By 1980, that had increased to 75 per cent. Now, it is more than 78 per cent. About 40 per cent of Spain's population live in only 10 cities.

As the nation prospered, people's standard of living rose. However, living standards and personal income did not rise uniformly across the whole country. While incomes in the cities are higher today than the European average, parts of Andalucia in the south and Extremadura in the west are amongst the poorest regions in the whole European Union.

## Back in Time

People first arrived in the Iberian peninsula 35,000 years ago. About 5000 BCE, they were joined by people from north Africa. Everyone lived in villages and cultivated the land. In about 1500 BCE, they started spreading from the coast into the interior. In 1100 BCE, Phoenicians from the area known today as Lebanon were the first Mediterranean people to arrive.

These stone houses and a village church, all with red-tiled roofs, are near Santillana, close to the northern coast of Spain. ▶▶

## Busy cities and quiet villages

Spain's cities are fast-paced, crowded, built-up, noisy and often congested with traffic. In city centres, the streets are lined with shops and offices. At night, the city streets are still busy as people go out for the evening.

Village life in the countryside is more peaceful and slower. There is less traffic and also less of the air pollution that goes with it. The streets are frequently narrow and winding, the buildings smaller, more picturesque and laid out in a less planned way. Goats and sheep are sometimes driven through the streets. Instead of supermarkets, local butchers, greengrocers, hardware stores and other small shops thrive.

The country's regions used to be easily distinguished by different styles of dress. Nowadays, suits, casual clothes or jeans and T-shirts, are worn everywhere. Traditional dress is only seen on special occasions such as weddings and fairs.

▲ In most cities, people live in blocks of flats or apartments or in houses in the suburbs. These are rented flats in Madrid.

Web Search ►►

► http://www.cia.gov/cia
  /publications/
  factbook/geos/
  sp.html

*Spain's entry in the CIA World Factbook, with data about the country and its people, government, economy, etc.*

# Farming and Fishing

Agriculture declined in Spain as people moved off the land into cities and other industries grew, but it is still an extremely important part of the Spanish economy, as is fishing.

One person in 12 works in agriculture. About 17 million hectares of land is cultivated, with 12 million hectares under permanent crops. More than half of the cultivated land lies in only three regions – Andalucia, Castilla y León and Castilla-La Mancha.

The main crops grown are cereals, especially wheat and barley, and rice. Spanish farming is less industrialized than in many other west European countries. Family-run farms dominate agriculture. Families account for two-thirds of the total agricultural workforce of 1.2 million.

**DATABASE**

## Livestock farming

| | |
|---|---|
| Cattle | 6.2 million |
| Sheep | 24.9 million |
| Goats | 2.9 million |
| Pigs | 22.0 million |
| Poultry | 42.0 million |

▲ Harvesting melons grown under plastic in Almeria on the southern coast.

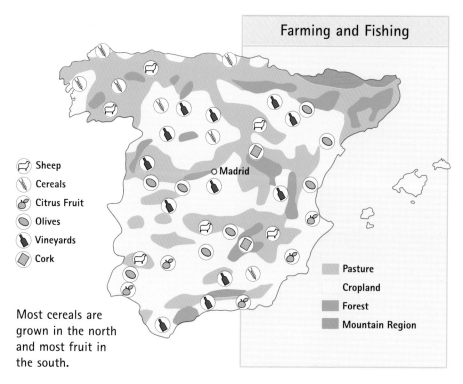

## Farming and Fishing

○ Madrid

- 🐑 Sheep
- 🌾 Cereals
- 🍊 Citrus Fruit
- 🫒 Olives
- 🍾 Vineyards
- ▱ Cork

Pasture
Cropland
Forest
Mountain Region

Most cereals are grown in the north and most fruit in the south.

## Commercial Fishing

Spain consumes more seafood per head of population than any other EU country. Its fishing fleet is bigger than all the other fishing fleets of Europe added together. It has 18,900 fishing vessels. Most of them fish in Spanish waters. The main fishing ports are Vigo and La Coruña.

◄◄ A fish auction in Santa Pola, a small town on the east coast.

## Web Search ►►

► http://countrystudies.us/spain
*Farming and fishing in Spain.*

► http://www.mapa.es/portada_en/htm
*Ministry of Agriculture, Fisheries and Food.*

## Wine and olives

Spain is one of the world's biggest wine producers. A million hectares of vineyards produce grapes for the wine industry. The wine most often associated with Spain is Rioja, named after the region where it is made. There are 40 wine-making regions in all. One of them, Jerez de la Frontera, is world-famous for the production of sherry.

More than 2 million hectares of land are planted with olive groves, mostly for the production of olive oil. The warm climate in the southern part of the country is ideal for growing citrus fruit, especially oranges, and early ripening produce such as tomatoes and avocados for export to northern Europe.

Barley is the main farming crop, followed by wheat and maize. ▼

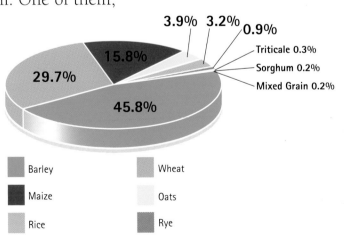

3.9%   3.2%   0.9%
Triticale 0.3%
Sorghum 0.2%
Mixed Grain 0.2%
15.8%
29.7%
45.8%

| | |
|---|---|
| Barley | Wheat |
| Maize | Oats |
| Rice | Rye |

# Resources and Industry

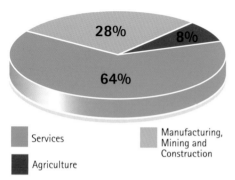

- Services
- Manufacturing, Mining and Construction
- Agriculture

▲ Proportion of workers in major industries. 'Services' increasingly grow while manufacturing declines.

28%

8%

64%

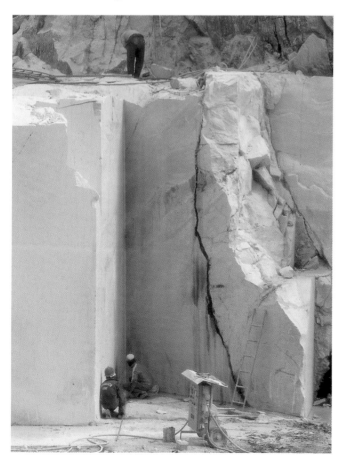

Spain is rich in mineral resources. It has large deposits of sulphur, mercury, nickel, copper, lead, phosphates and uranium. However, they often lie in folded or faulted rock around the edge of the Meseta Central, making them difficult to mine.

Coal is also an important mined resource. Mines in Asturias and along the Sierra Morena make Spain one of Europe's biggest producers of coal and lignite (a low-quality woody type of coal). Although Spain has substantial coal deposits, it has very little oil and natural gas resources. Most of its oil and gas needs are met by costly imports. As a result, Spain's economy has traditionally run a large trade deficit.

## Manufacturing and textiles

Spain's leading manufacturing industry is vehicle production. Most of the 3 million or so vehicles that are made each year are exported, with 90 per cent of them going to other EU countries. The country's steel and ship-building industries are facing serious competition from Japan and Korea, where production costs are lower.

The demand for tourist accommodation and a shortage of high-quality housing have produced a strong construction industry. Spain is a major producer and exporter of textiles and clothing. This earns the country more than £14 billion a year and provides employment for one in ten of the industrial workforce.

◄◄ Quarrying marble for the construction industry. Much of the marble is exported.

## Gross Domestic Product

As in many other developed countries, Spain's economy is dominated by services. In Spain's case, these are mainly tourism, finance and banking, retailing, telecommunications and transportation. Together, they account for about 64 per cent of the country's gross domestic product (GDP).

Oil tanker and refinery on the south-east coast. ▶▶

## Resources and Industry

 Car Manufacture

 Chemicals

Engineering

Fish Processing

Mining

Textiles

Tourism

Madrid ○

Spain's reserves of mercury are the world's largest. The country is also Europe's largest producer of high-grade iron ore, lead and zinc.

## Web Search ▶▶

▶ http://minerals.usgs.gov
*The website of the US Geological Survey, with details of the mineral reserves and mining output of different countries, including Spain.*

▶ http://minerals.usgs.gov/ minerals/pubs/country/ 2000/9438000.pdf
*A mineral map of Spain provided by the US Geological Survey.*

▶ http://www.trade. uktradeinvest.gov.uk/ clothing/spain
*Unemployment statistics for countries including Spain, provided by the United Nations Statistics Division.*

▶ http://www.eia.doe.gov/ emeu/cabs/spain.html
*Spanish energy industry.*

# Transport

Travel within Spain is generally quick and easy in most places thanks to the extensive road and rail networks, and air-links. The main roads and railway lines radiate out from Madrid to all other cities like the spokes of a wheel.

Spain's larger towns and cities are linked by buses and trains. Most rail services are provided by RENFE, the Spanish national railway company. Its *cercanias* (commuter trains) travel within and around major cities. *Regionales* (regional trains) travel between cities. *Largo recorrido* (long-distance) express trains provide long-distance services. Generally, small villages that do not have their own railway stations have bus services.

A large car and passenger ferry that sails between Spain's east coast and the Balearic Islands. ▼

## Transport

Spain's road and railway lines span the country and run along the coasts.

Spain has an extensive and modern transport system. As well as road, rail and air networks, there are navigable rivers and canals for boats and barges.

## Road and rail

In the past, Spain's mountain ranges presented formidable natural barriers to land transport. The construction of the first railways in the 19th century made it possible for people to travel long distances across the country more easily. Today, more than 500 million inter-city journeys and about 400 million local journeys are made every year by rail. The first motorways were built in the 1960s. Today, there are over 21 million cars on Spain's roads.

## Air and sea

Spain's national airline, Iberia, and a variety of other airlines provide international and internal air services. More than 40 of Spain's 110 airports handle commercial air traffic. Domestic flights carry 31 million passengers a year. With nearly 5,000 kilometres of coastline, Spain is heavily dependent on sea transport. It has one of the world's largest merchant fleets. The busiest ports are Bilbao, Algeciras, Tarragona and Barcelona.

### Web Search ▶▶

▶ http://www.renfe.es
*Website of the Spanish national rail service.*

▶ http://www.iberia.com
*Website of Iberia, the Spanish national airline.*

▶ http://www.trasmed iterranea.es
*The shipping line that carries passengers between Spain and the Balearic islands.*

# Education

Spain has a literacy rate of about 98 per cent thanks to its free and compulsory state education system.

Children enter primary school at the age of six, but they can attend *escuelas de Educación Infantil* (pre-primary school) before that. Basic primary and secondary education is free in state schools and compulsory up to the age of 16. Parents can also send their children to private schools, if they wish and can afford to. About one in three children attend private primary and secondary schools. Children attend school from Monday to Friday.

The school day generally starts at 10.00 a.m. and does not finish until 5.00 p.m. However, there is a long break of about two hours in the middle for the main meal of the day. Private schools and international schools sometimes start and finish their day earlier.

DATABASE

## Teaching qualifications

Teachers in pre-primary and primary schools must have a *Maestro* teaching diploma, awarded after three years at a university-level teacher training college. Secondary school teachers need a *Licenciado*, or an architecture or engineering degree, plus a teaching course.

Class in a state primary school in a suburb of Madrid. ▼

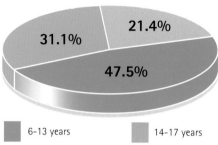

◄◄ Children boarding a bus for a primary school outing in Barcelona.

31.1%   21.4%

47.5%

■ 6-13 years          ■ 14-17 years

■ Higher Education
  (Universities, etc.)

▲
▲ Students in education, by age range or type of establishment.

## Further education

When students finish their compulsory education, they receive the *Graduado en Educación Secundaria* (certificate of secondary education). This enables them to go on to upper secondary education or vocational training. At the end of this, successful secondary students receive the *Bachiller* diploma. Successful students in vocational training receive the *Técnico* certificate.

The Bachiller diploma entitles students to go on to advanced vocational training or university. An entrance examination also has to be taken to enter some courses. The Spanish university system is one of the oldest in Europe. Some universities can trace their origins back to the Middle Ages. The oldest, at Salamanca, was founded in 1218. Madrid University dates from 1293.

In schools and universities in regions of Spain with their own language, classes are taught in both the official language, Castilian, and the regional language.

### Foreign Languages

Most Spanish children learn English or French as a foreign language. German is taught in some schools. As part of their language training, and with help from the EU higher education programme, many Spanish students spend part of their university courses in other European countries.

### Web Search ►►

► http://unstats.un.org/
  unsd/demographic/
  products/socind/
  illiteracy.htm
  *Literacy statistics for countries including Spain, provided by the United Nations Statistics Division.*

# Sport and Leisure

The climate in Spain makes golf and tennis popular all year round, with residents and tourists alike. Spain's own favourite sport is football.

Club football is dominated by two teams – Real Madrid and FC Barcelona. The best clubs regularly play in European competitions. Real Madrid has won nine European Championships since the 1950s. Spain's national football team reached the quarter-finals of the World Cup in 1998 and 2002.

Hundreds of golf courses have been built around the warm Mediterranean coast. This valuable resource has produced successful home-grown golfers. The best-known, Jose Maria Olazabal, has won tournaments all over Europe, the Middle East and the USA.

Sports enthusiasts all over the world turned their attention to Spain in 1992, when 10,500 athletes from 172 countries gathered in Barcelona for the summer Olympic Games.

### Bullfighting

Most towns have a bullring, where crowds gather to watch matadors fight, and kill, bulls. The spectators enjoy the spectacle of a courageous matador controlling a dangerous animal. It is seen as an art-form. However, many other Europeans condemn bullfighting as cruel.

A matador in action at a bullring in Seville. ▼

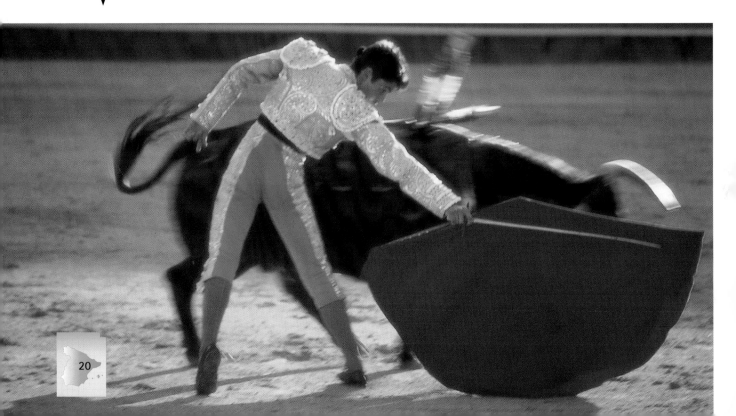

## Fishing and fiestas

Fishing continues to grow in popularity as a sport and leisure activity. Trout, salmon, pike, carp, barbel, tench and eels can be caught in many of Spain's rivers and lakes. Off the coast, sea anglers catch grey mullet, sea bream, bass, mackerel and tuna.

Every city, town and village in Spain has at least one *fiesta*, or festival. Many of them are held on holy days. The most famous fiesta is *San Fermín*, in Pamplona. Its highlight is the *encierro* (running of the bulls), when bulls are released to run through the crowded streets. One of the oddest fiestas is *La Tomatina* in Buñol, near Valencia, when 38,000 people hurl 130 tonnes of tomatoes!

### Pelota

The game of *pelota* (Spanish for ball) or *jai alai* ('merry festival') is particularly popular. Once played mainly in the Basque region in the north-east, it is now played all over Spain and in other parts of the world. Players wear a wicker scoop on one arm to catch the ball and fling it back to another player or against the wall of the court.

Numbers of Foreign Tourists

47,743,000    46,776,000    48,201,000

1998    1999    2000

▲ One in every ten tourists travelling outside their own country visit Spain.

A basketball match in the Olympic hall in Barcelona. ▼

### Web Search ►►

► http://www.realmadrid.com
*Website of the Real Madrid football club.*

► http://www.fipv.net/eng/eijuego/reglamentos.htm
*The game of pelota.*

► http://www.red2000.com/spain/toros
*The origins and history of bullfighting.*

Festival celebrations in Barcelona.

## Tapas and Paella

Eating out in restaurants and bars is very popular. Bars often offer small snacks called *tapas* to eat with a glass of wine or beer. They might be a few slices of cured ham, pieces of fish or octopus, chunks of sausage or salad vegetables. The dish most closely associated with Spain is *paella*, a mix of rice, saffron, meat and seafood.

*Semana Santa* (Easter Week) procession in Almería on the south coast. ►►

22

# Daily Life and Religion

Food is an important part of daily life in Spain. At lunchtime, while workers in many other European countries make do with a hurried sandwich, most businesses in Spain close for at least two hours.

Schools stop for a long lunch too. This long break for the main meal in the middle of the day is the famous Spanish *siesta*. Because of the siesta, the school day does not end until 5.00 p.m. and the business day does not usually end until about 6.45 p.m. Shops stay open to 8.00 p.m. or even later.

## Regional differences

The pattern of daily life is not the same all over Spain. The latest hours are kept in Madrid and the south of the country. Here, for example, the evening meal is not eaten until at least 10.00 p.m., often much later. Northern Spain tends to keep hours similar to the rest of Europe. Many big international corporations based in Spain are trying to adopt the same working hours as other businesses elsewhere in Europe but few have succeeded.

## Religion

Almost all Spanish citizens are Roman Catholic, although most do not attend church regularly. Catholicism was the country's official religion until 1978, when the new constitution broke the link between the state and the church. The constitution protects the citizen's right to religious freedom.

Spain was once a Muslim country and evidence of its Muslim history can still be seen today. The beautiful Grand Mosque stands in the middle of Córdoba. Parts of it date back to CE 796. And the magnificent 14th-century Alhambra in Granada was the palace-fortress of Spain's last Moorish rulers.

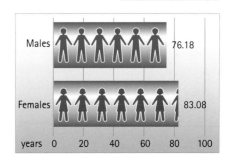

▲
▲ Spanish women live, on average, seven years longer than Spanish men.

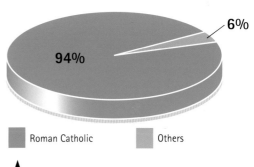

Roman Catholic    Others

▲
▲ The Spanish population is almost entirely Catholic.

Web Search ▶▶

▶ http://www.alhambra-patronato.es
*Website of the Alhambra, Granada.*

▶ http://www.alhambra-patronato.es/ingles/inforgenrl/informain.htm
*Information about food, drink, fiestas and traditions in Spain.*

# Arts and Media

### Gaudi

Some of the most dramatic buildings in Spain were designed by the Catalan architect Antonio Gaudi (1852-1926). His best-known work is the unfinished temple *Sagrada Familia* (Holy Family) in Barcelona. Gaudi died before the building was finished. Work restarted in the 1950s and continues today. *Sagrada Familia* is shown on the cover of the book.

### Cinema

Early Spanish film-makers like Luis Buñuel (1900-83) had to struggle against the repression of the Franco regime to get their films made. Cinema censorship ended in 1977. More recently, *The Others* (2001), starring Nicole Kidman, was made by the Spanish director Alejandro Amerábar, and the Spanish actors Antonio Banderas and Penelope Cruz are major Holywood stars.

$S$pain is renowned for its great artists and writers. Its rich musical tradition has also produced world-famous musicians, composers and singers.

Any list of the greatest artists of the last century would include the Spanish painters Pablo Picasso, Salvador Dalí and Joan Miró. One of Picasso's most famous works, *Guernica*, was inspired by the bombing of the Spanish town of the same name in 1937. The painting now hangs in the Centro de Arte Reina Sofia in Madrid along with other works of modern Spanish art.

Works by great Spanish artists of the past, such as Velázquez and Goya, are displayed in the Museo del Prado, also in Madrid. After the Prado and the Guggenheim Museum in Bilbao, Spain's most visited museum is the Museu Dalí in Figueres. It contains some of Dalí's works and the grave of the artist himself.

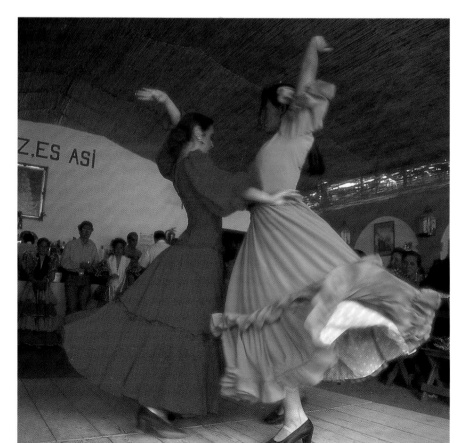

Flamenco dancers in Jerez. ▶▶

TV Broadcast Stations
(total 224)

 = 10 Stations

Radio Broadcast Stations
(total 924)

[radio icon] = 10 Stations

▲
▲ Spain's state television service, TVE, supplies 24 channels. There are many private and local TV and radio stations.

►► A view of the outside of the futuristic metal-clad Guggenheim Museum of Modern Art in Bilbao.

## Music and literature

Music is in the Spanish blood. Flamenco is a passionate style of folk dance and music associated with Andalucian Gypsies. Modern Spain has its own pop and rock bands. Young Spaniards enjoy the same, mainly American, music that is popular throughout the western world. The growing popularity of music with a Latin American flavour has helped to make Spanish artists such as Enrique Iglesias international stars.

Spain also has a long tradition of creative writing. Cervantes' book *Don Quixote*, first published in 1604, describes Don Quixote's adventures with his side-kick Sancho Panza. Spain is still producing writers of international importance. The novelist Camilo José Cela won the world's most prestigious literary prize, the Nobel Prize for Literature, in 1989.

🌐 **Web Search** ►►

► http://museoprado.mcu.es
*Website of the Prado Museum, Madrid.*

► http://www.salvador-dali.org
*Website of the estate of Salvador Dalí, with details of the three museums devoted to his work.*

► http://www.guggenheim-bilbao.es/idioma.htm
*The Guggenheim Museum in Bilbao.*

► http://www.spanish-fiestas.com/traditional/spanish-flamenco-dancing.htm
*The story of flamenco dancing.*

# Government

Spain is a constitutional monarchy. The head of state is a king, but real power lies with a government elected by the people.

The monarchy and democratic government were both restored in 1978, three years after the death of General Franco. Franco was a dictator who had ruled the country since winning power in a military coup in the 1930s.

Spain is divided into 17 *autonomías* (self-governing communities or regions). These are composed of a total of 50 provinces. At a level of administration below these, there are about 8,000 *municipios* (municipalities), each with its own mayor and council.

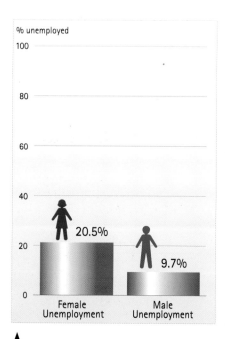

% unemployed

20.5% Female Unemployment

9.7% Male Unemployment

▲ Spain's traditionally high unemployment rate is falling fast, because new jobs are being created faster in Spain than anywhere else in the European Union.

Spain's autonomous communities have a high degree of independence from the central government which is based in the capital, Madrid.

 **ETA**

Since the 1960s Spain has been subjected to a campaign of violence by a terrorist group called ETA *(Euzkadi Ta Azkatasuna)*, meaning Basque 'Homeland and Liberty'. Its aim is to achieve independence for the Basque region. Peace talks in the 1990s won a temporary ceasefire, but ETA returned to violence in 2000.

The Basque people live not only in north-east Spain but also in the neighbouring region of France on the other side of the Pyrenees.

**Spain's Regions**

Galicia
Asturias
Cantabria
Basque Country
Navarra
La Rioja
Catalonia
Castilla y León
Aragón
Madrid
Madrid ○
Valencian Region
Extremadura
Castilla-La Mancha
Balearic Islands
Murcia
Andalucia
Canary Islands

Guards stand outside a government ministry building in the centre of Madrid.

## Monarchy and the Cortes

The monarch is the head of state, the commander-in-chief of the armed forces and the symbol of national unity. Since 1975, the monarch has been King Juan Carlos I.

The country is governed by the *Cortes Generales* (Parliament). It is bicameral, meaning that it is composed of two parts, or houses. These are the *Congreso do los Diputados* (Congress of Deputies) and the *Senado* (Senate). The Congress of Deputies is the more powerful of the two. Its 300 to 400 Deputies are elected by all citizens over the age of 18. The number of Deputies representing each province depends on its population. About four-fifths of the 259 senators are also elected. The rest are appointed by the self-governing communities (*autonomías*). The Parliament is elected for a maximum term of four years.

Until 1999, Spain's unit of currency was the *peseta*. On 1 January 1999, Spain was one of the first group of European Union countries to agree to give up their own currencies in favour of adopting a new currency, the euro. The transition was completed in January 2002.

**Web Search** ►►

► http://www.casareal.es
*Website of Spain's King and royal family.*

► http://www.congreso.
es/ingles/index.html
*The website of the Congress of Deputies, one of Spain's two houses of Parliament.*

► http://www.senado.es/
home_i.html
*The website of the Senate, Spain's second house of Parliament.*

# Place in the World

Spain is a successful modern democracy with a growing economy. It was the fifth largest economy in the EU in 2001. It is also the 16th largest exporting country in the world.

Spain was shunned by the international community during the Franco years. Since the end of this repressive era in the 1970s, it has formed closer ties with other countries and joined international organizations. Emigrants returning from abroad brought with them wealth and a desire for the consumer goods they had been accustomed to in other countries. As a result, economic growth in the country was rapid during the 1980s.

Spain maintains close contacts and trading links with many Latin American countries, especially Chile, Argentina, Brazil and Mexico. It is the single largest foreign investor in Latin America. However, most of its import and export trade is with other EU countries. It is also a member of important international organizations such as NATO (the North Atlantic Treaty Organization), the UN (United Nations) and the EU (European Union).

## International disputes

Spain has a long-running dispute with Morocco over the sovereignty of Spanish territories on and off the Moroccan coast. In 2002, Morocco landed troops on the tiny uninhabited island of Perejil. Spanish forces ejected them and, in a show of strength, sent warships to protect its coastal towns of Ceuta and Melilla.

## Gibraltar

Spain contests Britain's sovereignty over Gibraltar. Britain captured Gibraltar in 1704 and Spain formally handed it over to Britain in 1713. Spain tried to reclaim Gibraltar in 1963, but in 1967 the colony's 30,000 residents voted to remain British.

Spain closed its border with Gibraltar in 1969. It remained closed for 16 years. In 2002, Britain and Spain discussed sharing sovereignty over Gibraltar, a development that was very unpopular with its residents.

Every year, tourists flock to Spain's beaches, as here near Alicante.

## Columbus

In 1492, the Spanish king and queen financed Italian explorer Christopher Columbus to find a sea route to China and riches by sailing west from Europe. He failed but did discover America.

Spain's imports and exports.

EXPORTS
£91.3 billion
(Machinery, motor vehicles, foodstuffs, consumer goods)

IMPORTS
£117.5 billion
(Machinery and equipment, fuels, chemicals, semi-finished goods, foodstuffs, consumer goods)

## Web Search ►►

► http://news.bbc.co.uk/
1/hi/world/europe/
992004.stm
*Part of the extensive BBC News website featuring a timeline of modern Spain from the 1930s.*

## DATABASE

### Chronology of Historical Events from CE 1600

**1607**
Madrid made Spain's capital

**1701**
War of Spanish Succession begins when the king dies childless

**1714**
War of Spanish Succession ends with Philip V as king

**1821**
Spain gives independence to Mexico

**1824**
Spanish forces lose in Peru, ending Spanish rule in South America

**1898**
Spanish-American War. Spain loses control of Cuba, Puerto Rico and the Philippines

**1936-39**
Military coup and civil war brings General Franco to power

**1975**
Franco dies. King Juan Carlos I crowned

**1977**
First free election for 40 years

**1982**
Spain joins NATO

**1986**
Spain joins the EU

**1992**
Barcelona hosts Summer Olympics

**1996**
Right-wing Popular Party wins general election. Jose Maria Aznar becomes Prime Minister. He is re-elected in 2000

**2002**
Peseta replaced by euro

**Area:**
504,784sq km

**Population size:**
40,341,462

**Capital city:**
Madrid
(Population 5,100,000)

**Other major cities:**
Barcelona (pop. 1,510,000)
Valencia (pop. 781,000)
Seville (pop. 710,000)

**Longest rivers:**
Tagus (Tajo) (1,007 km)
Ebro (910 km)
Duero (895 km)

**Highest mountain:**
Teide Peak, Tenerife (3,718 m).
On Spanish mainland: Mulhacén
(3,481 m)

**Currency:**
euro
1 euro = 100 euro cents

**Flag:**
Three horizontal bands: red on
top, yellow in the middle, red at
the bottom. The national coat of
arms is on the flag-pole side of
the yellow band. The coat of arms

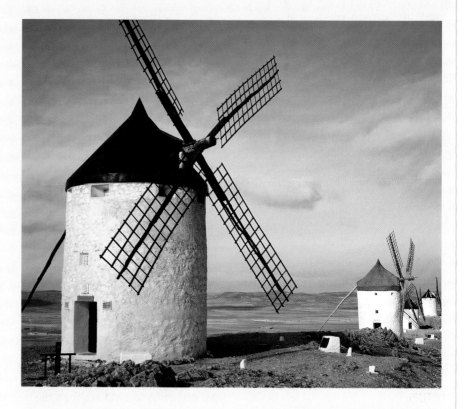

includes the royal seal between the
pillars of Hercules, representing the
two promontories, Gibraltar and
Ceuta, on each side of the eastern
end of the Strait of Gibraltar.

**Languages:**
Castilian (official language),
Catalan, Galician, Euskera (Basque).
Castilian is spoken by most of the
population.

**Major resources:**
Coal, lignite, gypsum, iron ore,
alumina, sulphur, sepiolite, potash,
pumice, feldspar, uranium,
magnesite, zinc, fluorspar,
strontium, barite, lead, peat,
copper, mercury, timber.

**Major exports:**
Machinery, motor vehicles, textiles,
foodstuffs, consumer goods, iron
and steel, petroleum products.

**National holidays and festivals:**
January 1: New Year's Day
January 6: Epiphany
May 1: May Day
July 25: St James's Day
August 15: Assumption
October 12: National Day
November 1: All Saints' Day
December 6: Constitution Day
December 8: Immaculate
Conception
December 25: Christmas Day

**Religions:**
Spain is almost entirely Roman
Catholic.

# Glossary

**AGRICULTURE**
Farming the land, including ploughing, planting, raising crops, and raising animals.

**ALTITUDE**
The height above sea level of a mountain or an area of land.

**CLIMATE**
The long-term weather in an area.

**CONTINENT**
One of the Earth's largest land masses: Europe, Asia, Australia, North and South America, Africa and Antarctica.

**COUP**
Short for *coup d'état*, a violent or illegal replacement of a country's government.

**CULTURE**
The beliefs, ideas, knowledge and customs of a group of people, or the group of people themselves.

**ECONOMY**
A country's finances.

**EMPIRE**
A group of peoples or territories ruled by one country.

**EXPORTS**
Products, resources or goods sold to other countries.

**GOVERNMENT**
A group of people who manage a country, deciding on laws, raising taxes and organizing health, education, transport and other national systems and services.

**GROSS DOMESTIC PRODUCT**
The value of all goods and services produced by a nation in a year.

**IMPORTS**
Products, resources or goods brought into the country.

**LITERACY**
The ability to read and write.

**LITERACY RATE**
The percentage of the population who can read and write.

**MANUFACTURING**
Making large numbers of the same things by hand or, more commonly, by machine.

**PENINSULA**
Land projecting into the sea from the mainland so that it is almost an island.

**POPULATION**
All the people who live in a city, country, region or other area.

**POPULATION DENSITY**
The average number of people living in each square kilometre of a city, country, region or other area.

**RESOURCES**
Materials that can be used to make goods or electricity, or to generate income for a country or region.

**RURAL**
Having the qualities of the countryside, with a low population density.

**SPANISH ARMADA**
A fleet of warships sent against England in 1588 by Philip II of Spain.

**URBAN**
Having the qualities of a city, with a high population density.

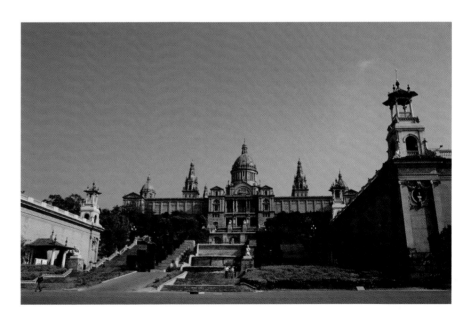

# Index